FRIENDS
OF ACPL

D1712935

THE RIGHT MOVES

Preparing for Dance Competitions

Pam Chancey

The Rosen Publishing Group, Inc., New York

Special thanks to Maria DiDia

Special thanks also to International Dance Challenge

Published in 2004 by The Rosen Publishing Group, Inc.
29 East 21st Street, New York, NY 10010

First Edition

Library of Congress Cataloging-in-Publication Data

Chancey, Pam.
The right moves : preparing for dance competitions / Pam Chancey.— 1st
ed. p. cm. — (The curtain call library of dance)
Contents: Starting off on the right foot—A competitive spirit—It's
your body—The competition's on—The right attitude.
ISBN 0-8239-4559-6 (lib. bdg.)
1. Dance—Competitions—Juvenile literature. [1. Dance. 2. Contests.]
I. Title. II. Series.

GV1596.5.C53 2004
792.8—dc22

                                                        2003014340

Manufactured in the United States of America

CONTENTS

INTRODUCTION

You eagerly wait backstage at your region's most important dance competition. You're charged from head to toe with excitement. Finally, the judges call the name of your dance routine. You've been rehearsing it for months. *Am I ready?* you ask yourself. Before you can answer the question, the lights go up and the music starts. You're on! The competition begins!

As you dance onstage, you feel the heat from the lights. You feel aglow. You sense the gaze of the judges who are seated in front of you. *Do they like what they're seeing?* You watch their expressions as you move through the dance steps that you know so well. You hear the audience applaud after your big leap across stage. You're pumped! When you hold your final pose, the room fills with the cheers of the crowd. You're on top of the world, knowing you did your best. It feels great to be a competitive dancer!

From auditioning to performing, this book will lead you through the fun-filled journey that is the world of dance competitions. It will help you get the most out of your adventure and be a successful dance competitor. So get ready…let's dance!

● Many dance competitions feature different categories such as jazz, tap, modern, and ballet. Just remember to have fun in whichever category you perform!

CHAPTER 1

STARTING OFF ON THE RIGHT FOOT

Dance competitions began in the 1960s. Their goal was to challenge professionals and add prestige to the art of dance. At that time, many people criticized dance competitions for attempting to turn dance, an art form, into a "sport." Today, however, public opinion has changed and there are over 1,000 dance competitions and conventions across the United States each year. However, the road to becoming a competitive dancer doesn't start at conventions, or even at the competitions. It starts with you making the commitment.

Taking dance lessons after school is a popular extracurricular activity. Many young dancers take one or two classes per week. However, if you want to compete in dance, a more serious approach to your training is required. Fine-tuning your dance skills with extra classes and rehearsals will help prepare you for the world of dance competitions. First you have to audition for the competitive team at your studio. Then you rehearse your routine to perfection and mentally prepare for the thrilling day of competition.

Making the Team

Many studios invite students to audition for their dance company, or team. Auditions are usually held in the summer

● At times, competition among dancers can be tough. These young dancers are waiting their turn to show their skills at a dance audition.

or early fall season. If you are invited to audition, you will want to show that you are serious about making the team. Good attendance at your weekly classes is an important way to do this. It demonstrates your commitment to training. Be at every class, on time, and prepared. You may also want to ask your teacher if there are extra classes or workshops you can take. This shows that you're eager to improve. Always dress your best, too! Proper dance attire such as a leotard or tights is a must in class and especially at an audition. Do not wear baggy clothes. Dancing "full out" will show your teacher that you'll be an asset to his or her team.

You may not make the competition team after your first audition. Regardless of the

Team Tip

Competition choreographer Ashlie Solomon suggests that you ask your teacher if you can understudy or be an apprentice with the competition team. This will show your interest in the opportunity to compete in the future.

results, however, don't get discouraged. There are numerous reasons why you may not make the cut. Age, height, and previous experience are all aspects of the selection process. There is always a "next time," so keep your enthusiasm for dance alive!

Preparing for Your First Competition

Congratulations! You've made the team and you're on your

● Participating in workshops can be a great way to improve your dancing. It also shows your teacher that you are eager to do what it takes to make the team.

Tips From Young Competitors

Competitor Allison Holly, age thirteen, says, "It doesn't matter if the judges think you are the best, as long as you know you tried your best at the competition!" Adrienne Hicks, a competitor since age seven, says, "Now that I am fourteen, I think the most important thing is to believe in yourself—and know you're not going to win them all!" First-time competitor McCall Scofield, age ten, says, "If you have a good attitude, dance competition is neat because you meet a lot of new people and you learn cool stuff." Katherine Welling, a national dance competition winner, says, "You can't base your hard work on the opinion of judges. You have to learn it's not about the trophy, it's about your love for dance!"

9

● Remember to stay focused so that you can learn all the moves your new routines may require.

way to becoming a competitive dancer. Be ready to move forward. Before rehearsals begin, get your parents involved. Your studio will inform you of the competition schedule. Make sure your family is ready to dedicate weekends for rehearsals and travel time for competitions. Their support is essential in making your journey a success. Your parents will also need to know of any required fees for costumes, rehearsals, and entries. Some studios plan fund-raisers such as bake or flower sales to help pay for competitions.

Any dance performance requires preparation. However, rehearsing for dance competition involves additional time and effort. Your teacher will want your team's routine to be challenging and precise. You may have to learn new turns, tricks, and more difficult dance techniques. Try not to get frustrated! The next few months may be tough, but you'll have tons of fun along the way.

What Goes On at a Dance Competition

Participating in a dance competition is exciting! Dance competitions are fun, energy-packed events that are often held over a weekend. They usually take place in your community or in a nearby town. Some national competitions may require you to

Rehearsal Tip

Ask your teacher if you can videotape your competition rehearsals so that you can practice your routine at home.

11

travel to an out-of-state destination. There are often more than 100 routines scheduled for the event. Dancers ages five to twenty line up to test their talents and show their technical skills. Most competitions allow dancers to perform on a stage and to receive critiques and awards based on their performance.

Practice Makes Perfect

Preparing a dance routine for a competition takes some time. Through extra rehearsals, your dance teacher will "polish" the moves so that everyone in your group looks and performs alike. Precision moves are difficult, especially if you are in a large group. Be prepared to practice the same "eight counts" over and over again,

until it's exactly as your teacher envisions it. Being patient with teammates and supportive of your teacher's work ethic will make the journey more enjoyable for everyone.

Staying on Top of It All!

Managing your busy schedule is a key to success. Here are a few quick tips:

• Schoolwork comes first.
• Bring your textbooks to the studio in case you have a break between rehearsals.
• Try to get homework done before dance classes each afternoon.
• Keep an academic planner handy and write down due dates.
• Plan ahead for time-consuming projects like book reports or science fairs.

● Being a part of any team means work-ing closely together. However, a success-ful group dance routine requires a very high level of precision and uniformity.

CHAPTER 2

A COMPETITIVE SPIRIT

According to Nancy Raffa, International Ballet Competition Gold Medalist, "It's the preparation for competition that makes you improve. It's a learning experience that allows you to get on stage." She adds, "It gives you encouragement and keeps you working for better things."

Once rehearsals for the competition are underway, you'll need to prepare mentally for the big event. That begins with preparing to be a good winner—or a good loser. You need to be ready to accept the outcome of the competition, whether you win or lose.

To assure that you keep positive goals in mind, your parents, teachers, and fellow dancers must also have good attitudes. Good-spirited competition with your peers is a normal and healthy way of expressing yourself, making new friends, and learning valuable lessons about life. Competition can be great fun—but winning isn't everything.

Before you leave for the competition, prepare yourself for some situations that may arise by asking yourself some important questions.

What If My Team Loses?

Everyone should try to be a good winner and a graceful loser in all aspects of life!

● Everyone likes to win at a dance competition. However, a good competitor knows there are more valuable lessons to be gained from the competition.

However, with the right attitude, no one loses in dance. Dance is an expressive art form that is rewarding in any setting. Don't let a trophy or award stand as the judge of your love for dance. Keep in mind the critique and strive to make your next performance even stronger. If your team loses, you will still probably receive some type of award. Even if you receive the lowest score of the day, accept the award with honor and be thankful for the experience.

How Are My Parents Involved?

You will look to your parents for support throughout your dance experience. Generally, parents understand the challenging lifestyle you've chosen. However, some parents become overwhelmed with the competition atmosphere and add even more pressure. Parents, teachers, and competitors must discuss this subject beforehand. Decide how you will *all* accept a win or a defeat. Then, when it comes time to compete, everyone

● There are many different awards presented at a competition. Yet, remember that you perform because you love to dance—and not just to win trophies and ribbons.

will be ready to enjoy the experience in a positive "spotlight."

What If I Compete Against Friends?

There is enough winning to go around for everyone! Competing against friends is hard, but it's an opportunity to grow as a dancer. Learn to cheer for everyone. Support your friends and wish them luck!

Packing and Preparing for the Competition

Packing and preparing for competition requires thought and organization. Take your time! Organize your suitcase or bag so you can find everything easily. Your teacher will make a checklist of all of your costume parts and pieces. Try not to forget an important part of your outfit, such as a hat, prop, or gloves.

Sample Packing Checklist

- Dance outfit(s) and shoes
- Quick-fix supplies such as safety pins, thread and needle
- Aspirin or aspirin substitute, for head or muscle aches
- Towel
- Hairbrush, hair spray, and other hair-care products
- Makeup and makeup removers
- Pen or pencil and paper, to keep track of the lineup
- CD or audio cassette of your music
- Portable CD or cassette player

● Why make your parents be in charge of packing your bag? Taking charge of your own suitcase is a useful lesson in responsibility!

Who Are the Judges? What Are They Looking For?

When you're on stage at the competition, you will see a panel of judges seated in front of you. Usually three to five judges will watch your routine. The judges come from a variety of backgrounds such as professional dancers, teachers, choreographers, or directors. They want to help you! A judge's job is to positively critique your routine. They will give you advice on how to better perform your moves. This is called constructive criticism.

Generally, you will be judged in three areas: technique, choreography, and performance. Technique scores are based on your execution of technique. For example, if you are performing a ballet routine, the judges will grade you on how well you point your feet or align your arms based on classical ballet technique. Choreography scores are based on how well your routine flows together. The judges want to see what creative steps your teacher has

● These dancers are competing in the small groups category. Their routine has the kind of energy and style that the judges like to see.

taught you and how expressively you perform them. Performance scores are based on your personality on stage, costuming, and knowledge of the routine. The judges want to see you dance with energy and enthusiasm!

Combined, these scores will reflect which award your team receives. Some competitions award gold, silver, and bronze awards while others give first, second, or third places. Whichever award your team receives, remember that if you did your very best, you are a winner!

● The best reason to be involved in any group competition is to have fun. This group of friends is simply having a blast.

● Being a gracious winner is a point of pride for any serious competitor.

CHAPTER 3

IT'S YOUR BODY

A carpenter swings a hammer, a painter strokes a brush, and a dancer uses his or her body as an instrument to perform. Eating well and using proper stretching techniques will keep you "on your toes" for your journey in competitive dance.

Your dancer's body is important, so take care of it! Knowing what snacks and meals are better for your body type will give you extra boosts of energy. Warming up and stretching on a regular basis will enhance your flexibility. Conditioning will build good habits and guide you toward a healthy lifestyle. Healthy dancers will "glow" on stage, whereas a dancer who doesn't take care of his or her body will often be on the sidelines recovering from injuries.

Eating Healthily

We all have to eat—and we must eat well! Food is the fuel

Food Tip

Supplements can NEVER replace healthy foods. Power bars and "quick fixes" are great to throw in your dance bag when you are in a rush, but there is nothing that can substitute for a well-balanced meal.

● For breakfast, a bowl of cereal with milk is a great source of carbohydrates, calcium, and vitamins. Just add some fruit, and you'll be off to a great start each and every day!

that drives our bodies. We would never expect a car to run if the gas tank was empty, so we can't expect our bodies to run without fuel either.

Breakfast is the meal that will jump-start your day. Eat a balanced breakfast that includes grains, protein, and fruit. Drinking lots of water is vital to a dancer's diet, too. It is recommended that you drink at least 8 ounces of water between each dance class to prevent dehydration. So grab a water bottle and keep it with you!

Power Snacks

On a daily basis, planning healthy snacks for after-school cravings is essential for keeping your energy up during dance classes. Packing whole-grained breads or fruit will satisfy you until dinner and will keep you away from the candy machines and fast food stops.

At the competition, it is often hard to find convenient restaurants or concessions. Emily Robinson, a dance competitor, recommends being prepared by packing nutritious snacks in your travel bag.

Warm-Up

Proper warm-up is not only necessary for stretching your muscles and avoiding injury. It also relaxes your body and calms those jittery nerves before you go on stage. You may want to get an early start on warming up at the competition by walking or jogging around the performance area. Simply taking a brisk tour up and down the hallways heats the large muscles and gets your blood circulating. Next, experts suggest stretching slowly—do not bounce. Keep breathing deeply and hold stretches for 30 seconds each. Then relax.

Heads up! Exercising and Stretching on Your Own

In addition to regular dance classes each week, you may want to condition your body on your own. Activities such as running, swimming, riding your bicycle, or playing sports are great ways to get exercise. You may also want to try yoga, Pilates, or aerobic classes to work on your flexibility. Exercising, stretching, and staying active will not only greatly improve your dance ability, but also will help you stay healthy—mentally and physically. Exercise helps build stronger bones and muscles. It also can improve your memory and your focus. Keeping fit reduces stress and helps you sleep easier.

Keep It Clean!

When you work out hard, as you do when you dance, your body needs to keep itself cool. Sweating is your body's natural way of doing this.

● Yoga is a great way to improve your flexibility. It also helps you learn to use your breathing to help you relax.

25

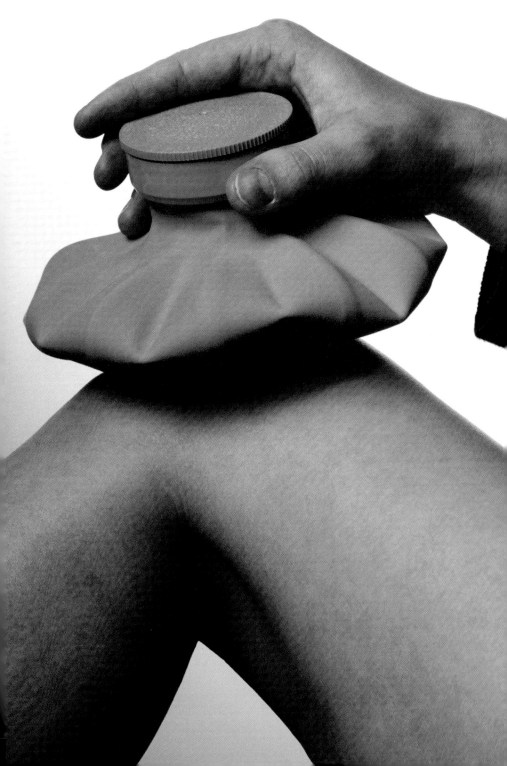

However, you want to stay fresh and clean. Keep your dance clothes clean and shower every day. Wash your face and feet after rehearsals and competitions. Finding a good deodorant to wear while dancing can help you keep your cool when things get hot.

Injury Prevention

Be careful! Extended practice, exhaustion, or heightened nerves may weaken your body. This can make you especially susceptible to injury. So, do not overdo it! If you happen to pull or strain a muscle, there are key steps you may want to follow to help you recover quickly. Many dancers use the "RICE" rule:

Rest - Sit down immediately.
Ice – Wrap ice in a towel and apply it to the injury.
Compression – Use a bandage or other fabric to wrap the ice pack firmly around the injured body part.
Elevation – Prop up the injured body part so that it is higher than your heart to limit any swelling.

Then get an appointment with your doctor as soon as possible!

● Applying ice to an injury reduces the blood flow to that area. This helps minimize swelling and reduces the pain.

CHAPTER 4

THE COMPETITION IS ON!

You've worked hard to polish your routine. You've put your all into preparing for the day of the competition. Finally that day is here!

Group Effort

Most competitions have various categories that you can enter. They are Solo, for a single dancer; Duo-Trio, for two to three dancers; Small Groups, for up to eight dancers; Large Groups/Lines, for nine or more dancers; and Production Numbers, which are for more than fifteen dancers. No matter what category your team is in, it's crucial to work as a group.

Master teacher and judge Frank Hatchett reminds dancers that, "Being part of a competition ensemble takes total commitment. Each dancer is responsible for his

Going Solo

It's an honor to be invited to compete in a solo. Working one-on-one with your teacher will improve your confidence and your skills. Listening to the judges' critique of your solo is also excellent advice—the comments are meant specifically for you. Share them with your teacher and use them to better your dance development. Just remember: There is no room for divas! Support your fellow solo competitors as well as your group. A chain is only as strong as its weakest link—in dance and in attitude!

or her part of the choreography, emotionally and technically. Remember that you are part of a team and the judges and audience have to feel the team energy."

A Teacher's Job

Your dance teacher may be one of your favorite role models. You can count on him or her to offer you and your group support in dance classes, rehearsals, and at the competition. Your teacher will help prepare you for the stage and will cheer you on throughout the experience. Although you may look to your teacher for guidance, try to remember he or she may be very busy on the competition day. Your teacher is in charge of registering your

● Your teacher works hard to help you become the best dancer and competitor that you can be. Listen to your teacher when he or she gives instruction.

studio and working with the competition staff. Your team or parents can schedule a time to "run through" your dance, do makeup, and stretch before your call time. This will free up your teacher to organize a smooth day at the competition. Your teacher wants you to do your best. He or she has to put a lot of effort into your routine and you'll want to make him or her proud! Oh, and don't forget to thank him or her for getting you there!

Convention Classes

In addition to the competition events, some competitions offer classes. These classes may be held before, during, or after the competition. They are typically held in large ballrooms at a hotel or in auditoriums. The teachers for these classes may also be your judges at the competition! Convention classes are great opportunities because they offer you new styles of dance in a new environment.

Are You a Good Member of the Audience?

Watching the competition before you go on stage is encouraging and will boost your morale. You'll see dancers performing under the bright lights and you'll grow even more excited to "show your stuff"! Being a good and supportive member of the audience is important at the competition. Applaud for every routine, even if it's not one from your studio. Remember that you'll be on stage soon and you'll wish for the same support in return.

Calming Your Nerves

It's almost your turn! You've watched several routines performed. Your group has met to practice, you have properly stretched and touched up your makeup. Now you're ready to go on. However, you may be nervous. Yet being nervous can be a *good* thing! You can channel your nervous energy to enhance your performance. Here are some tips to help you calm your nerves and prepare for your performance:

First, get familiar with your environment. If you're given permission, check out the backstage area to locate your entrance and exits. This way, you'll be ready when it's your turn.

Secondly, have a group pep talk. Huddle together and wish each other good luck. Hold hands and unite one last time—as a team.

Finally, take a moment for yourself and, most important, don't forget to breathe!

Backstage Manners

During your brief time backstage, you'll see many dancers changing costumes, stretching, and practicing. Try not to get distracted by others. Stay focused on your routine. Your teacher will want you to stay with your teammates and not wander off. Sometimes, the competition lineup will run out of order (due to quick costume changes), so listen up and be ready to dance at any time!

Audience Tip

Most competitions don't allow dancers to sit in the audience in their costumes. So you may want to bring a cover-up. A suggested cover-up would be a large button-down shirt.

CHAPTER 5

THE RIGHT ATTITUDE

Attitude and Respect

Performing at a dance competition is an experience that can give you lots to think about. Now that you've competed, determine for yourself if competitive dance is about an award or about the journey to receive it. Many people believe that the lessons you learn on your way to a goal are more important than actually accomplishing that goal.

For example, pretend you are a swimmer on an Olympic team who has trained since you were very young. During your final stages in the training process, you travel all over the world refining your skills. You work with some of the best coaches and see amazing facilities. However, the week before the Olympics, you pull a muscle and you don't get to go to the games. You are filled with disappointment. Yet, aren't you a better swimmer than you've ever been? Hasn't your experience taught you things about your abilities, strengths, and weaknesses? If you compete in dance, you've already accomplished goals and learned how your body, mind, and spirit all work together.

After the Results Come In

You hang your medal on your dresser and your trophy stands tall on your shelf. You're proud to have tried your best. No matter what "number" is written on the award, it's a treasure! Any trophy, medal, or plaque is a nice, visual reward for your hard work. Now, be prepared to return to dance class at your studio after the competition to review what happened.

If you won, you'll celebrate and reflect on the points in the routine that made it great. However, there is still more to learn. Dance is an art form and perfection is an ideal to work toward, not a reality to achieve. You can always practice and improve.

If your team lost the competition, or did not do as well as you'd hoped, try not to let the defeat get you down. Your

● Whether it is the first medal you ever win or the prize trophy you've been striving for, there are always new goals to set and new lessons to be learned.

teacher will study the judges' critiques and may consider revisions in the routine. If you competed in a solo, you may want to take home the score sheets to study the suggestions the judges made. In your group routine, teamwork and respect for your teacher are needed now, more than ever.

You're a Role Model

As a respected member of the competition team, many dancers at your studio will look up to you. You're a "leader" to the young dancers and noncompetitive students. Cherish that role—it is a delicate job! The young dancers may want to be just like you one day. Show them what it takes. Other dancers observe your class attendance, dress, and attitude.

Actions Speak Louder Than Words

Showing your teacher that you're a dedicated student is important. Staying in class reinforces your commitment to her and to your team. Don't skip class just because the competition is over. There are always upcoming shows, recitals, and competitions. Consistent training is important for your health and your

Keep It Positive!

Try not to become involved with gossip. Do your best to find something positive in everyone. No matter what happened at the competition, be sure to let everyone at the studio know all of the great things that came along the way!

growth as a dancer. No matter how many times you practice the same routine, keep a positive attitude while rehearsing!

Saying "Thank You"

Your dance teachers and competition directors work

● Showing a positive attitude in class is one way of saying thanks to your teacher.

long hours. Many teachers sacrifice time with their own families to direct competition teams. Your parents have also been supportive. They're the ones who have given you this opportunity to dance and compete. Remember to say "thank you" to your teachers and parents throughout your journey.

Lesson Learned

Life skills are learned every day. Applying what you learned is smart. The skills you acquire being a competitive dancer are not only useful on stage, but also in daily life. Let's review some of the lessons learned along our journey to and from a dance competition.

• COMMITMENT is a pledge to do something in the future. It is important to commit to your audition, your team, and your teacher. You'll find that committing to most anything is necessary to succeed. For example, we must commit to our schoolwork and studies in order to graduate and further our education.

• TEAMWORK is an important skill that you'll use in any sport, study group, and, one day, at your job. Learning how to work with others and gain their trust makes you a stronger individual.

• RESPONSIBILITY for our actions must be assumed. Keeping up with your studies, practicing hard, and eating healthily are examples of being responsible.

• ATTITUDES are part of your personality. It's often hard to keep a positive attitude, especially in the face of defeat. Everyone wants to be around someone with a good attitude. Believing in yourself will show in your performance and in your character!

• APPRECIATION for your teachers, family, and friends must never be forgotten. Taking lessons, and especially competing in dance, is a great opportunity. Therefore, everyone appreciates a simple "thank you" in words or actions.

● Through competition you learn a lot about yourself and your teammates. Keep pushing each other to grow and you may find friendships that last a lifetime.

GLOSSARY

apprentice (uh-**pren**-tiss) Someone who learns a trade or craft by working with a skilled person.

audition (aw-**dish**-uhn) A short performance by a dancer, singer, actor, or musician to see whether he or she is suitable for a part in a play, concert, or other events.

choreographer (kor-ee-**og**-ruh-fur) A person who creates ideas and movements for dance.

commitment (kuh-**mit**-muhnt) A pledge or obligation to follow a certain course of action.

compete (kuhm-**peet**) To try hard to outdo others at a task, race, or contest.

critique (cri-**teek**) The act of pointing out good and bad points of a performance.

dehydration (dee-**hye**-dray-shuhn) The state in which you do not have enough water in your body.

energy (**en**-ur-jee) The strength to do active things without getting tired.

exhaustion (eg-**zawst**-shuhn) The state of being extremely or completely tired by overwork.

nutritious (noo-**trish**-uhss) Containing substances that your body can use to help stay healthy and strong.

role model (**rohl mod**-uhl) A person whose behavior in a particular role is imitated by others.

sacrifice (**sak**-ruh-fisse) To give up something important or enjoyable for a good reason.

strive (**strive**) To make a great effort to do something.

susceptible (suh-**sep**-teh-buhl) Open or subject to some stimulus or influence.

FOR MORE INFORMATION

Organizations

Dance/USA
1156 15th Street, NW, Suite 820
Washington DC, 20005-1726
(202) 833-1717
Web site: http://www.danceusa.org

School of American Ballet
70 Lincoln Center Plaza
New York, NY 10023-6592
(212) 769-6600
Web site: http://www.sab.org

Web Sites

Due to the changing nature of Internet links, the Rosen Publishing Group, Inc., has developed an online list of Web sites related to the subject of this book. This site is updated regularly. Please use this link to access the list:

http://www.rosenlinks.com/ccld/comp/

FOR FURTHER READING

Books

Hamilton, Linda H. *Advice for Dancers: Emotional Counsel and Practical Strategies.* New York: John Wiley & Sons, Inc., 2002.

Jacob, Ellen. *Dancing.* New York: Variety Arts Books, 1999.

Magazines and Publications

Curtain Call Dance Club Revue
P.O. Box 709
York, PA 17405-0709
Web site: http://www.cckids.com

Dance
333 7th Avenue, 11th floor
New York, NY 10001
(212) 979-4803
Web site: http://www.dancemagazine.com

Dancer
2829 Bird Avenue, Suite 5 PMB 231
Miami, FL 33133
(305) 460-3225
Web site: http://www.danceronline.com

Dance Spirit
Lifestyle Ventures, LLC
250 West 57th Street, Suite 420
New York, NY 10107
(212) 265-8890
Web site: http://www.dancespirit.com

BIBLIOGRAPHY

"Behind the Judges' Table." Editorial. Angelo Moio: *Dance Teacher Magazine*, December 2002, pp. 56-58

"Essentials of Dance Competitions." Editorial. Aria Nosratinia, www.ee.princeton.edu/~aria/comp _tips.html

Gaede, K., et al. *Fitness Training for Girls.* San Diego, CA: Tracks Publishing, 2001

"Jump-Start Your Day." Editorial. Elaine Magee, MPH, RD: *Dance Spirit Magazine*, February 2003, pg. 65

Kent, A., et al. *The Dancers' Body Book*. New York: HarperCollins Publishers Inc., 1984

Kirberger, Kimberly. *No Body's Perfect*. New York: Scholastic, Inc., 2003

"This Dance Competition Does More Than Give Prizes." Editorial. Jennifer Dunning: *The New York Times*, January 1985

INDEX

About the Author

Pam Chancey began dancing at age three and first competed at age eight. In high school, she began teaching dance. In college, she founded a competitive dance company that competed across the country. She currently judges and teaches on faculty at regional and national dance conventions. She is also a director and teaches on faculty at the prestigious Broadway Dance Center in New York City.

Editor: Kevin Somers **Book Design:** Christopher Logan and Erica Clendening

Developmental Editors: Nancy Allison, CMA, RME, and Susan Epstein